THE LITTLE CHICKEN COOKBOOK

THE LITTLE

CHICKEN

COOKBOOK

SMITHMARK

This edition first published in 1996 by
SMITHMARK Publishers
a division of US Media Holdings Inc.
16 East 32nd Street
New York, NY 10016

© 1996 Anness Publishing Limited

Produced by Anness Publishing Limited
1 Boundary Row
London SE1 8HP

SMITHMARK books are available for bulk purchase for
sales promotion and for premium use. For details write or call
the manager of special sales, SMITHMARK Publishers, a
division of US Media Holdings Inc., 16 East 32nd Street,
New York, NY 10016; (212 532 6600)

ISBN 0-8317-7423-1

Publisher Joanna Lorenz
Senior Cookery Editor Linda Fraser
Assistant Editor Emma Brown
Designers Patrick McLeavey & Jo Brewer
Illustrator Anna Koska

Photographers Amanda Heywood, James Duncan,
Steve Baxter, Edward Allwright & Karl Adamson
Recipes Carla Capalbo, Laura Washburn,
Shehzad Husain, Catherine Atkinson, Hilaire Walden, Steven
Wheeler, Christine France, Shirley Gill, Alex Barker,
Sarah Gates & Sue Maggs

10 9 8 7 6 5 4 3 2 1

Printed in Singapore by
Star Standard Industries Pte Ltd

Contents

Introduction

Low in fat, high in protein, affordable, convenient and infinitely versatile, chicken is the perfect choice for family meals, picnics, parties, barbecues and intimate dinners. There's a cut for every occasion, from inexpensive wings (delicious with a spicy coating) to tender breasts. Thighs make excellent and economical casseroles, drumsticks beg to be barbecued and ground chicken, while not as flavorsome as some other ground meats, makes an interesting filling for a pie, casserole or loaf, especially when partnered with other ingredients. Whole birds can be roasted, stewed, or boned and stuffed to make a stunning centerpiece which will certainly be the talk of your dinner table.

Squabs – originally wildfowl, but now raised on farms like chickens – weighing around 1 pound or so are perfect for single portions. Cornish game hens, with their all-white meat and mild gamey flavor, weigh twice as much and are perfect for 2 people.

Since most of the fat on a chicken is concentrated under the skin, use skinned portions wherever possible. If you prefer to leave the skin in place, for extra flavor in a soup or stew perhaps, skim off as much fat as possible from the surface of the finished dish.

In terms of economy, it is often better to buy one or two whole birds, and cut them into serving pieces, than to take the more convenient option of choosing prepacked portions. Two fresh chickens will furnish enough breasts, wings, thighs and drumsticks for at least three family meals – and the carcass or carcasses will also provide

6

the basis for a nourishing stock or soup. Cut-up chicken is more perishable than whole birds, so freeze any surplus.

When speed is the determining factor, prepacked chicken comes into its own. Boneless, skinless breasts are a real boon to the busy cook. Baked, broiled or sliced for a stir-fry, they are the ideal fast food; in fact, care must be taken not to overcook them, or they will be dry and rubbery.

Chicken is universally popular, and every nation has its own favorite recipe, from Indonesia's spicy Chicken Satay to France's classic casserole, Coq au Vin. Many such dishes feature in this book, including Tandoori Chicken, Broiled Chicken with Melon & Cilantro Salsa, Chicken & Prawn Jambalaya and Spicy Chili Chicken.

Tempted to try something new? Why not? Perhaps chicken's only failing is its familiarity. We serve it so often that there's a danger of taking it for granted. Most of us stick to a fairly small selection of tried and trusted recipes, except when we are entertaining, and seldom seek out new soups, starters or main courses. The Little Chicken Cookbook aims to inspire – recipes range from mouthwatering morsels like Chigarillos and Chicken Goujons to special occasion treats such as Lemon Chicken with Guacamole and Cornish Game Hens Veronique. You'll find plenty of suggestions for salads, soups, terrines and kebabs, plus a comforting curry and a tasty old-fashioned chicken pie Grandma would have been happy to serve.

Take a fresh look at chicken – and try a little tenderness.

Chicken Cuts

BREAST

Chicken breasts are sold both on and off the bone, with or without the skin. The meat is especially tender.

LEG

A large bone-in portion of chicken consisting of the thigh and drumstick, the leg is usually casseroled.

SUPREME

A French term to describe a boneless, skinless chicken breast. Suprêmes often include the wing joint.

THIGH

A popular cut for casseroling, thighs are either sold whole, with skin, or boned and skinned for stuffing and rolling.

WING

Although there is very little meat on a wing, it is generally tender and succulent. Wings are usually marinated and then barbecued or fried, and are good value.

DRUMSTICK

The lower part of the chicken leg, between the thigh and the foot. Drumsticks are very popular for barbecuing. They can also be crumbed or dipped in batter and deep fried.

SCALLOP

This is a skinless, boneless slice of chicken breast, cut diagonally against the grain. The term is also used for a whole boneless breast which has been placed between sheets of clear film and beaten until thin.

FILLET

The smaller of the two parts that make up a chicken breast, the fillet may be removed for cooking separately, but is more usually left in place.

Types of Chicken

STEWING CHICKENS

These are about ten months and over and weigh between 4–6 pounds. They require long and slow cooking to make them tender; around 2–3 hours.

CAPONS

These are castrated cock birds which grow very large and tender. They usually weigh about 6–8 pounds.

CORNFED CHICKENS

These are free-range birds, and are generally more expensive. They usually weigh about 2½–3 pounds.

CORNISH GAME HENS

These birds are not chickens, but a cross-breed of Cornish gamecocks and Plymouth Rock hens, which accounts for their mild, gamey flavor. Unlike chicken, they have all-white meat. Cornish game hens weigh about 2 pounds and serve two people.

SQUABS

The smallest of these birds, which can weigh less than 12 ounces, are called "doves," when grown up a little, and weighing 1¼ pounds or so, they are known as "pigeons." Larger squabs are enough for one person, but you will need to serve two of the smaller birds per person.

ROASTERS

These birds weigh between 3½–5 pounds and will easily feed a family.

BROILERS

These tender birds weigh about 2½ pounds and will serve three to four people.

FRYERS

Larger than broilers, about 2½–3½ pounds. Fryers will serve up to six people.

Techniques

BONING A BREAST

Remove the skin. With the thinner side of the breast facing you, cut down carefully between the flesh and the bone, keeping the blade of the knife very close to the bone. Work the tip of the knife around the breastbone and ribs until the breast can be removed in a single piece.

BONING A THIGH

Remove the skin. With the smooth side of the thigh down, make a deep cut down to the bone and along its length, keeping the knife blade close to the bone and easing the flesh away with your fingers. Work the tip of the knife around the bone to scrape away any flesh adhering to it. As soon as it is possible to do so safely, grip the end of the bone and cut around the base of it so that the bone can be removed.

Note: Instructions for boning a whole bird are given in the recipe for Ballotine of Chicken on page 28.

STUFFING A CHICKEN

Stuff a chicken immediately before cooking. Only stuff the neck end of the bird, not the large body cavity. Pack the stuffing in lightly, then form the chicken into a neat shape, tucking the neck flap under to hold the stuffing in place, and holding down with the wing tips. Alternatively, using your hands, ease the skin away from the breast to create a pocket, then spoon in the stuffing. Smooth the chicken skin over, at the same time pressing the stuffing out so that it forms a thin, even layer. Skewer the skin to the bird to hold the stuffing in place, if necessary.

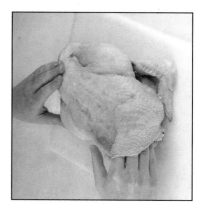

TRUSSING A WHOLE CHICKEN

With the bird on its back, push a skewer through the chicken below the thigh bone. Turn it on to its breast and loop the string around the wings, crossing it over to hold them firmly in place. Pass the string under the ends of the skewer and crisscross it over the back of the chicken. Turn the bird over and bring both ends of the string up to tie the drumsticks together firmly.

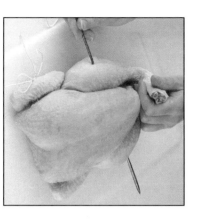

FOOD SAFETY TIPS

• Chill fresh chicken as soon as possible after purchase, storing it in the coldest part of the refrigerator. Ensure that it cannot drip on to any food beneath.

• Wash boards, knives and your hands very thoroughly after preparing chicken and before touching any other food.

• Thaw frozen chicken fully before cooking, and never refreeze raw chicken after thawing. Never thaw chicken in warm water to save time.

• Do not partially cook chicken, intending to finish cooking it later. Bacteria can continue to multiply in uncooked areas, even if the bird is kept chilled.

• Always cook chicken right through. Test roast chicken by piercing the thickest part of the thigh with a skewer; the juices should be clear.

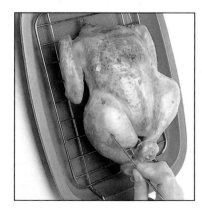

Appetizers & Light Meals

Chigarillos

INGREDIENTS

10-ounce package of filo pastry
3 tablespoons olive oil
Italian parsley, to garnish

FILLING

12 ounces ground raw chicken
1 egg, beaten
½ teaspoon ground cinnamon
½ teaspoon ground ginger
2 tablespoons raisins
1 tablespoon olive oil
1 small onion, finely chopped
salt and ground black pepper

SERVES 4

1 Make the filling. Place the chicken, egg, spices and raisins in a bowl. Heat the oil in a frying pan, and fry the onion until tender. Cool, then add to the bowl, and stir the mixture well. Add salt and pepper to taste. Preheat the oven to 350°F.

2 Grease a baking sheet. Keeping the filo sheets together, cut them into 10 x 4-inch strips, and cover with a damp dish towel to prevent the pastry from drying out.

3 Remove one filo strip, and brush it lightly with oil. Place a small spoonful of filling about ½ inch from the end, fold in the sides, then roll the strip up neatly to make a small cigar shape. Place on the prepared baking sheet. Repeat with the remaining strips. Brush the chigarillos with oil, and bake for about 20–25 minutes until golden brown and crisp. Serve hot, garnished with the parsley.

Chicken Goujons

Ingredients

4 chicken breasts, skinned and boned
3 cups fresh white bread crumbs
1 teaspoon ground coriander
2 teaspoons paprika
½ teaspoon ground cumin
3 tablespoons flour
2 eggs, beaten
oil for deep-frying
salt and ground black pepper
lemon wedges and fresh cilantro, to garnish

Dip

1¼ cups plain, strained yogurt
2 tablespoons lemon juice
4 tablespoons chopped fresh cilantro
4 tablespoons chopped fresh parsley

Serves 8

I Make the dip by mixing the ingredients in a small bowl. Cover, and refrigerate. Divide each chicken breast into two fillets. Sandwich the fillets between sheets of plastic wrap, and use a rolling pin to flatten to a thickness of ¼ inch.

2 Mix the bread crumbs with the spices and a little salt and pepper in a shallow bowl. Put the flour in a separate bowl or strong plastic bag, and put the beaten egg in a third bowl.

3 Cut the pieces of chicken into 1-inch strips. Toss them in the flour, pat off any excess, then coat each strip in turn, first in egg, and then bread crumbs.

4 Heat the oil for deep-frying in a heavy-bottomed pan. Fry the goujons in batches until golden and crisp, then drain on paper towels, and keep hot while cooking successive batches. Serve the goujons hot, garnished with the lemon wedges and cilantro. Offer the yogurt and herb dip separately.

Thai Chicken Soup

INGREDIENTS

1 tablespoon sunflower oil
1 garlic clove, finely chopped
2 large chicken breasts, skinned, boned and diced
½ teaspoon ground turmeric
¼ teaspoon hot chili powder
¼ cup coconut cream
4 cups hot chicken broth
2 tablespoons fresh lime or lemon juice
2 tablespoons crunchy peanut butter
2 ounces thread egg noodles, broken into short lengths
1 scallion, finely chopped
1 tablespoon chopped fresh cilantro
salt and ground black pepper

GARNISH

2 tablespoons shredded coconut
½ red chili, seeded and finely chopped

SERVES 4

1 Heat the oil in a large saucepan. Fry the garlic until pale gold, then add the chicken and spices. Fry, stirring, for 3–4 minutes more.

2 Pour the coconut cream into the hot chicken broth in a pitcher. Stir until combined, then add to the saucepan with the lime or lemon juice, peanut butter and egg noodles. Mix well.

3 Bring to a boil, stirring, and then cover, and simmer for 15 minutes. Add the scallion, cilantro and plenty of salt and pepper. Cook for 5 minutes more.

4 Meanwhile make the garnish by browning the coconut lightly with the chili in a small ungreased frying pan. Stir the mixture constantly. Serve the soup in heated bowls, sprinkled with the browned coconut garnish.

Nutty Chicken Bites

12 ounces ground raw chicken
½ cup pistachios, finely chopped
1 tablespoon lemon juice
2 eggs, beaten
flour, for coating
¾ cup chopped blanched almonds
¾ cup dried bread crumbs
salt and ground black pepper
fresh cilantro, to garnish

LEMON SAUCE
⅔ cup chicken broth
7 ounces cream cheese
2 teaspoons lemon juice
1 tablespoon chopped fresh parsley
1 tablespoon snipped chives

SERVES 4

1 Mix the chicken, nuts and lemon juice in a bowl. Stir in half the beaten egg, and add salt and pepper to taste. Shape the mixture into 16 balls of equal size. Toss the balls in flour to coat them lightly but evenly, patting off any excess.

2 Pour the remaining egg into a shallow bowl. Spread out the almonds and bread crumbs on separate sheets of foil. Coat the balls in egg, almonds and finally bread crumbs, pressing the coating on well. Refrigerate until ready to cook.

3 Preheat the oven to 375°F. Arrange the balls on some well-greased baking sheets, and bake for 15 minutes or until golden brown, crisp and cooked right through.

4 In the meantime make the lemon sauce. Gently heat the chicken broth with the cream cheese, whisking until smooth. Add the lemon juice and fresh herbs, with salt and pepper to taste. Serve the chicken bites on individual plates, garnished with the cilantro, and surrounded with the lemon sauce.

Chicken, Bacon & Walnut Terrine

INGREDIENTS

2 chicken breasts, skinned and boned
½ slice of bread, crust removed
1 egg
1 large garlic clove, crushed
12 ounces bacon, ground or
finely chopped
8 ounces chicken livers, trimmed and
finely chopped
¼ cup chopped walnuts, toasted
2 tablespoons sweet sherry or Madeira
½ teaspoon ground allspice
½ teaspoon cayenne pepper
pinch each of grated nutmeg and ground cloves
8 bacon strips
salt and ground black pepper
Belgian endive leaves and chives, to garnish

SERVES 8–10

2 Preheat the oven to 400°F. Stretch the bacon strips on a board using the back of a broad-bladed knife. Neatly line a 1½ pounds loaf pan with the bacon strips, cutting them to fit where necessary. Spoon in half the ground bacon mixture, and arrange the chicken strips on top. Cover with the remaining bacon mixture, smoothing the surface. Cover the pan with lightly greased foil, seal well, and press down firmly

3 Place the terrine in a roasting pan, and pour in enough boiling water to come halfway up the sides of the loaf pan. Bake for 1–1½ hours, until the juices run clear when the terrine is pierced with a skewer, and it is firm to the touch.

4 Remove the terrine from the oven, take off the foil, and drain any excess fat or liquid. Cover with fresh foil, place weights on top of the terrine, and set aside to cool completely.

5 When cold, remove the terrine from the pan, cut into thick slices, and serve, garnished with the Belgian endive leaves, chives and walnut pieces.

1 Cut the chicken breasts into thin strips, and season lightly. Soak the bread in the egg in a bowl. Mash with the garlic, then add the ground or chopped bacon, and mix well, using your hands to distribute the bacon evenly. Add the chopped chicken livers, walnuts, sherry or Madeira and spices, with plenty of salt and pepper. Mix well.

Chicken Liver Pâté

INGREDIENTS

1 cup butter
12 ounces chicken livers, trimmed
2 garlic cloves, crushed
1 teaspoon chopped fresh sage
1 tablespoon Marsala, brandy or medium
dry sherry
salt and ground black pepper
fresh sage, to garnish
Melba toast, to serve

SERVES 4

1 Melt about 2 tablespoons of the butter in a frying pan. Add the chicken livers and garlic, and fry over moderate heat for 5 minutes or until the livers are firm but still pink in the middle. Then turn all the mixture into a food processor or blender.

2 Add 10 tablespoons of the remaining butter to the frying pan, and heat until melted, stirring occasionally. Pour into the processor or blender, and add the sage and Marsala, brandy or sherry. Process until smooth, then season to taste.

3 Divide the pâté between four individual pots or ramekins, smoothing the surface. Melt the remaining butter in a clean pan, and pour it over the pâté to seal. Either garnish each pot with two sage leaves, refrigerate until set, and serve in the pots, or scoop out of the pots, and serve garnished with fresh sage. Serve with triangles of Melba toast.

Chicken Satay

INGREDIENTS

4 chicken breasts, skinned and boned
lettuce leaves, to serve
4 scallions and 8 lemon wedges, to garnish
SATAY SAUCE
½ cup crunchy peanut butter
1 small onion, chopped
1 garlic clove, crushed
2 tablespoons pickle
4 tablespoons olive oil
1 teaspoon light soy sauce
2 tablespoons lemon juice
¼ teaspoon chili powder

SERVES 4

1 Combine all the ingredients for the satay sauce in a food processor or blender. Process until smooth, then scrape the mixture into a large, shallow dish.

2 Cut the chicken into 1-inch cubes. Add to the satay sauce, and stir to coat. Cover the dish with plastic wrap, and refrigerate for 4 hours or preferably overnight to allow the flavors of the sauce to penetrate the chicken.

3 Put 8–12 wooden satay skewers in water to soak for about 30 minutes. Preheat the broiler or prepare the barbecue. Thread the cubes of marinated chicken onto the drained satay skewers, reserving the sauce. Cook the skewers for 10 minutes, turning once, and brushing occasionally with the reserved satay sauce.

4 Serve each portion on a bed of lettuce, garnished with a scallion and two lemon wedges.

Classic Dishes

Chicken Cordon Bleu

INGREDIENTS

4 chicken breasts, skinned and boned
4 slices cooked lean ham
4 tablespoons grated Swiss cheese
2 tablespoons olive oil
1 cup button mushrooms, sliced
4 tablespoons white wine
salt and ground black pepper
watercress, to garnish
green beans and baked potatoes, to serve

SERVES 4

1 Sandwich each chicken breast between sheets of plastic wrap, and use a rolling pin to flatten each fillet to a thickness of ¼ inch.

2 Lay a slice of ham on each chicken breast, and trim the ham to fit. Sprinkle one half of each ham-topped breast with grated cheese, and season with a little salt and pepper. Fold each breast carefully in half, and secure with a wooden toothpick.

3 Heat the oil in a frying pan, and brown the chicken breasts on both sides. Transfer to a platter, and keep hot. Add the mushrooms to the oil remaining in the pan, and cook over high heat for 3–4 minutes to brown lightly. Return the chicken to the pan, and pour over the wine. Cover, and simmer for 15–20 minutes until tender. Transfer to heated plates, remove the toothpicks, and garnish with watercress. Serve with green beans and baked potatoes.

Old-fashioned Chicken Pie

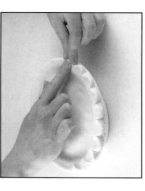

INGREDIENTS

1 chicken, about 4–4½ pounds
1 onion, quartered
1 tarragon or rosemary sprig
1¼ cups water
2 tablespoons butter
1 cup small button mushrooms
2 tablespoons flour
4 ounces cooked ham, diced
2 tablespoons chopped fresh parsley
1 pound fresh or thawed frozen puff pastry
1 egg, beaten
salt and ground black pepper

SERVES 4

1 Preheat the oven to 400°F. Put the chicken in a casserole, with the onion, herb sprig and water. Cover with a lid, and bake for 1¼ hours or until the meat is tender.

2 Transfer the chicken to a plate, and remove the skin. Strain the cooking liquid into a pitcher or bowl. Set aside to cool. Remove the meat from the chicken bones, cutting it into large chunks.

3 Melt the butter in a saucepan. Cook the mushrooms for 2–3 minutes. Meanwhile skim off any fat from the surface of the chicken stock. Add water to make the stock up to 1¼ cups.

4 Sprinkle flour over the button mushrooms, then gradually stir in the chicken stock. Bring to a boil, stirring, then add the ham, chicken and parsley, with salt and pepper to taste. Turn into one large or four individual pie dishes, and set aside to cool.

5 Roll out the pastry on a lightly floured surface to a round or oval about 2 inches larger than the pie dish. Cut a narrow strip to place around the edge of the dish, brush it lightly with beaten egg, then fit the lid in place. Scallop the edges, and knock up the sides with the back of a knife. Cut a hole in the center of the pie(s) to allow the steam to escape. Decorate with pastry leaves.

6 Heat the oven to 400°F again. Glaze the pastry with beaten egg. Bake until well risen and golden brown. Individual pies will require 25–35 minutes and a large pie 35–45 minutes.

Tandoori Chicken

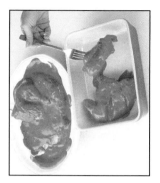

INGREDIENTS

1 cup plain yogurt
1 teaspoon garam masala
2-inch piece of fresh ginger, peeled and
finely chopped
2 garlic cloves, crushed
1½ teaspoons chili powder
¼ teaspoon ground turmeric
1 teaspoon ground coriander
1 tablespoon lemon juice
1 teaspoon salt
2 tablespoons corn oil
few drops of red food coloring (optional)
4 chicken quarters, skinned

GARNISH

mixed salad leaves
lime slices
tomato quarters
fresh green chilies, halved

SERVES 4

1 Mix the yogurt, garam masala, ginger, garlic, chili powder, turmeric, ground coriander, lemon juice and salt in a bowl. Add the oil and red coloring, if using, and mix well. Cut two slits in the flesh of each chicken quarter, and place in a single layer in a shallow dish. Spoon the yogurt marinade over, cover, and marinate for about 3 hours.

2 Preheat the oven to 475°F. Transfer the chicken from the marinade to an ovenproof dish. Bake for about 20–25 minutes or until the chicken is cooked right through, and has begun to brown on top. Serve the chicken on a bed of mixed salad leaves, garnished with some lime slices, tomato quarters and halved green chilies.

Coq au Vin

INGREDIENTS

3 tablespoons flour, seasoned

1 chicken, about 4–4½ pounds, cut into 8 joints

1 tablespoon olive oil

4 tablespoons butter

20 shallots

3-ounce piece of bacon, rind removed, diced

about 20 button mushrooms

2 tablespoons brandy

1 bottle red Burgundy wine

1 bouquet garni

3 garlic cloves, roughly chopped

1 teaspoon light brown sugar

1 tablespoon butter, softened

1 tablespoon flour

salt and ground black pepper

chopped fresh parsley and croûtons, to garnish

SERVES 4

1 Place the seasoned flour in a strong plastic bag, add each piece of chicken in turn, and shake to coat. Heat the oil and butter in a large flameproof casserole. Sauté the shallots and bacon for about 3–4 minutes, until the shallots have browned lightly. Add the mushrooms, and fry for 2 minutes. Using a slotted spoon, transfer the bacon and vegetables to a bowl.

2 Add the chicken pieces to the hot oil remaining in the casserole. Cook for 5–6 minutes. Pour in the brandy, carefully ignite it, then shake the pan gently until the flames subside. Add the wine, bouquet garni, garlic and sugar, and season to taste. Bring to a boil, lower the heat, cover, and simmer for 1 hour, stirring occasionally. Return the shallots, bacon and mushrooms to the casserole, replace the cover, and simmer for 30 minutes more.

3 Using a slotted spoon, transfer the chicken, vegetables and bacon to a heated serving dish. Keep hot. Remove the bouquet garni, then boil the liquid in the casserole rapidly until reduced slightly. Cream the butter and flour together, then whisk small amounts of this mixture into the sauce to thicken it slightly. Pour the sauce over the chicken mixture, and garnish with parsley and croûtons.

Ballotine of Chicken

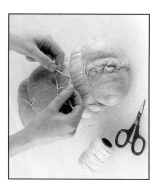

INGREDIENTS

1 chicken, about 4–4½ pounds
watercress, to garnish
STUFFING
4 tablespoons butter
1 onion, finely chopped
12 ounces ground pork
4 ounces rindless bacon strips, chopped
1 tablespoon chopped fresh parsley
2 teaspoons chopped fresh thyme
2 cups fresh white bread crumbs
2 tablespoons sherry
1 large egg, beaten
¼ cup pistachios
12 pitted black olives
salt and ground black pepper

SERVES 8

1 Bone the chicken. Use a small, sharp knife to remove the wing tips (pinions), then turn the chicken onto its breast. Slit down the length of the backbone. Cut the flesh away from the carcass, scraping the bones clean. Carefully cut through the sinew around the leg and wing joints, and scrape down the bones to free them. Remove the carcass, taking care not to cut through the skin along the breast bone.

2 Make the stuffing. Cook the onion in half the butter until soft. Turn into a bowl, mix in the remaining ingredients, and add salt and pepper to taste.

3 Preheat the oven to 350°F. To stuff the chicken, lay it flat, skin side down, and level the flesh as much as you can. Shape the stuffing down the center of the chicken, then fold the sides over the stuffing, and sew neatly together, using a needle and dark thread. Tie with fine string into a roll.

4 Place the roll, joint down, on a rack in a roasting pan. Melt the remaining butter, and spoon it over the roll. Bake for 1¼ hours or until cooked (the juices should run clear when the meat is pierced with a skewer), basting often. Set aside to cool completely before removing the string and thread. Wrap in foil, and refrigerate. Serve in slices, at room temperature, garnished with watercress.

Traditional Roast Chicken

INGREDIENTS

1 chicken, about 4–4½ pounds
2 tablespoons butter, softened
4 rindless bacon strips
2 tablespoons oil
2 tablespoons flour
1¼ cups chicken broth or vegetable water
watercress sprigs, to garnish
broiled small link sausages and
bacon rolls, to serve
PRUNE & NUT STUFFING
2 tablespoons butter, softened
½ cup pitted prunes, chopped
½ cup chopped walnuts
1 cup fresh white bread crumbs
1 egg, beaten
1 tablespoon chopped fresh parsley
1 tablespoon snipped chives
2 tablespoons sherry or port
salt and ground black pepper

SERVES 4

1 Preheat the oven to 375°F. Mix all the stuffing ingredients in a bowl, seasoning well. Using two-thirds of the stuffing, stuff the neck end of the chicken quite loosely. Shape the rest of the stuffing into small balls. Set aside.

2 Tuck the neck skin under the chicken to secure the stuffing, and hold in place with the wing tips. Place the chicken in a roasting pan, spread with the butter, and cover the breast with the bacon strips. Roast for 1½–2 hours, basting every 30 minutes. Test by piercing the thickest part of the thigh with a sharp knife or skewer; the juices should run clear. Transfer the cooked chicken to a heated platter, cover with tented foil, and set aside to rest in a warm place while you cook the stuffing balls and make the gravy.

3 Heat the oil in a small frying pan, and fry the stuffing balls until browned and cooked through. Keep hot. Discard most of the fat from the roasting pan, leaving the residue. Transfer to the stove, and sprinkle over the flour. Cook until golden brown, stirring constantly, then gradually stir in the broth or vegetable water. Heat, stirring, until the gravy boils and thickens. Add salt and pepper to taste.

4 Garnish the chicken with watercress, and serve with the the stuffing balls, sausages and bacon rolls. Pour the gravy into a warmed sauce boat, and serve with the chicken.

Lunches and Suppers

Sweet & Sour Kebabs

INGREDIENTS

2 chicken breasts, skinned and boned
8 pickling onions or 2 medium onions, peeled
4 rindless bacon strips
3 firm bananas
1 red bell pepper, seeded and diced
Italian parsley, to garnish

MARINADE

2 tablespoons brown sugar
1 tablespoon Worcestershire sauce
2 tablespoons lemon juice
salt and ground black pepper

HARLEQUIN RICE

2 tablespoons olive oil
generous 1 cup cooked rice
1 cup cooked peas
1 small red bell pepper, seeded and diced

SERVES 4

1 Mix together the marinade ingredients. Cut each chicken breast into four even-size pieces, add to the marinade, and cover. Set aside for at least 4 hours or preferably overnight.

2 Blanch the onions in boiling water for 5 minutes, and drain. If using medium onions, cut them into quarters using a sharp knife.

3 Cut each bacon strip in half. Peel the bananas, and cut each into three pieces. Wrap a strip of bacon around each banana piece. Thread onto metal skewers with the chicken pieces, onions and pepper pieces. Brush with the marinade. Broil or barbecue for 15 minutes, turning and basting with the marinade. Keep hot while you prepare the rice.

4 Heat the oil in a frying pan, and add the rice, peas and pepper. Stir until heated through. Serve with the kebabs, garnished with flat leaf parsley.

Bacon-wrapped Chicken Roulades

INGREDIENTS

4 chicken thighs, skinned and boned
4 ounces frozen chopped spinach
1 tablespoon butter
⅓ cup pine nuts
pinch of ground nutmeg
½ cup fresh white bread crumbs
4 rindless bacon strips
2 tablespoons olive oil
⅔ cup chicken broth
2 teaspoons cornstarch mixed with
4 teaspoons water
2 tablespoons light cream
1 tablespoon snipped chives
salt and ground black pepper
salad leaves, to garnish

SERVES 2

I Preheat the oven to 350°F. Sandwich the chicken thighs between sheets of plastic wrap, and flatten them with a rolling pin. Heat the spinach with the butter in a pan until thawed, then cook rapidly, stirring occasionally, until dry.

2 Remove the pan of spinach from the heat. Stir in the pine nuts, nutmeg and bread crumbs, with salt and pepper to taste. Divide the mixture among the pieces of chicken, roll up neatly, and wrap each roll in a bacon strip. Secure with string.

3 Heat the oil in a frying pan. Brown the rolls all over, then transfer to a shallow baking dish. Pour over the broth, and bake for 15–20 minutes until tender.

4 Transfer the chicken rolls to a serving plate, remove the string, and keep hot. Strain the cooking liquid into a pan, and stir in the cornstarch mixture and cream. Heat, stirring all the time, until the mixture thickens. Adjust the seasoning, and add the chives. Serve the sauce with the roulades on individual plates. Add a salad garnish.

Balti Chili Chicken

INGREDIENTS

SERVES 4–6

5 tablespoons corn oil
8 large green chilies, slit
2 onions, chopped
½ teaspoon mixed onion seeds (kalonji) and
cumin seeds
4 curry leaves
½-inch piece of fresh ginger, grated
1 teaspoon chili powder
1 teaspoon ground coriander
1 garlic clove, crushed
1 teaspoon salt
4 chicken breasts, skinned, boned and cubed
1 tablespoon lemon juice
1 tablespoon chopped fresh mint
1 tablespoon chopped fresh cilantro
8–10 cherry tomatoes
naan bread or parathas, to serve

1 Heat the oil in a deep round-bottomed frying pan or medium karahi. Lower the heat slightly, and fry the chilies until the skin starts to change color.

2 Add the onions to the pan, and fry for 3–4 minutes, then stir in the mixed onion and cumin seeds, curry leaves, ginger, chili powder, ground coriander, garlic and salt. Fry for a few seconds, stirring.

3 Add the chicken cubes, and toss over the heat for 7–10 minutes until the chicken is cooked through, and the onions are tender.

4 Sprinkle the lemon juice over the top, and add the mint and cilantro. Dot with the cherry tomatoes, and cook until warmed through. Serve at once, with naan bread or parathas.

COOK'S TIP

The whole chilies make this a very hot and spicy dish. If you prefer a milder flavor, use only four chilies, and remove the seeds.

Broiled Chicken with Melon & Cilantro Salsa

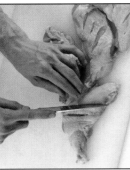

INGREDIENTS

4 chicken breast portions, breast bones removed
pinch each of celery salt and cayenne pepper
2 tablespoons corn oil
corn chips, to serve
fresh cilantro, to garnish

SALSA

10 ounces watermelon, seeded and diced
6 ounces cantaloupe melon, seeded and diced
1 small red onion, finely chopped
1–2 green chilies, seeded and finely chopped
4 tablespoons chopped fresh cilantro
2 tablespoons fresh lime juice
pinch of salt

SERVES 4

1 Preheat the broiler. Slash the chicken portions at intervals with a sharp knife. Place on a rack over a broiler pan, and season with celery salt and cayenne. Brush with the oil, and broil for 15 minutes or until golden and cooked through, turning once.

2 Meanwhile, to make the salsa, mix all the diced melon with the onion, chilies, cilantro and lime juice in a bowl. Stir lightly, and season with salt.

3 Place the bowl of salsa on a large platter. Arrange the corn chips and broiled chicken pieces around it, and garnish with cilantro. Serve the dish immediately.

Chicken with Asparagus

INGREDIENTS

4 large chicken breasts, skinned and boned
1 tablespoon ground coriander
2 tablespoons olive oil
1¼ cups chicken broth
20 slender asparagus spears, trimmed
1 tablespoon cornstarch mixed with
2 tablespoons water
1 tablespoon lemon juice
salt and ground black pepper
1 tablespoon chopped fresh parsley, to garnish

SERVES 4

1 Divide each chicken breast into two fillets. Sandwich the fillets between sheets of plastic wrap, and use a rolling pin to flatten them to a thickness of ¼ inch. Cut the fillets diagonally into 1-inch strips. Place the ground coriander in a bowl or strong plastic bag, add the chicken strips, and toss to coat them lightly.

2 Heat the oil in a large frying pan. Fry the chicken in batches over high heat for 3–4 minutes until lightly colored. As each batch cooks, season it with salt and pepper, then use a slotted spoon to transfer it to a plate. Keep the chicken hot.

3 When all the chicken is cooked, add the chicken broth to the fat remaining in the pan. Stir to incorporate any residue on the bottom, then add the asparagus spears. Cook for 3–4 minutes, or until they are tender.

4 Move the asparagus to one side of the pan, and stir the cornstarch mixture and lemon juice into the chicken broth in the pan. Heat, stirring constantly, until the sauce thickens. Return the chicken to the pan, spoon the sauce over it, and reheat gently. Serve on individual heated plates, garnished with chopped parsley.

Herb Crumbed Chicken Breasts

INGREDIENTS

4 chicken breasts, skinned and boned
1 tablespoon Dijon mustard
1 cup fresh white bread crumbs
2 tablespoons chopped fresh parsley
1 tablespoon dried mixed herbs
2 tablespoons butter, melted
salt and ground black pepper
new potatoes and mixed salad, to serve

1 Preheat the oven to 350°F. Arrange the chicken breasts in a single layer on the base of a greased baking dish. Spread with the Dijon mustard, and season.

2 Mix the bread crumbs and herbs in a bowl, sprinkle the mixture evenly over the chicken breasts, and press down gently to coat. Drizzle with the melted butter.

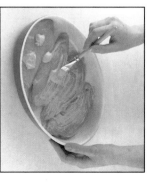

3 Bake the crumbed breasts uncovered for 20–25 minutes, until the coating is crisp, and the chicken is tender. Serve at once, with new potatoes and mixed salad, if liked.

Stir-fried Sweet & Sour Chicken

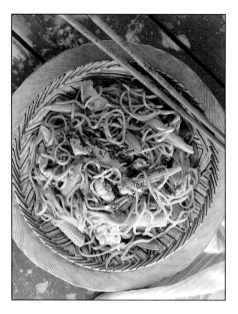

INGREDIENTS

10 ounces Chinese egg noodles
2 tablespoons vegetable oil
3 scallions, chopped
1 garlic clove, crushed
1-inch piece of fresh ginger, peeled and grated
1 teaspoon hot paprika
1 teaspoon ground coriander
3 chicken breasts, skinned, boned and sliced
4 ounces sugar snap peas, trimmed
4 ounces baby corn, halved
8 ounces fresh bean sprouts
1 tablespoon cornstarch
3 tablespoons soy sauce
3 tablespoons lemon juice
1 tablespoon sugar
3 tablespoons chopped fresh cilantro, to garnish

SERVES 4

1 Bring a large saucepan of lightly salted water to a boil. Add the egg noodles, and cook according to the instructions on the package until tender. Drain, cover, and keep hot.

2 Heat the oil in a wok or large frying pan. Add the scallions, and cook gently for 2 minutes.

3 Mix in the garlic, ginger, paprika and the coriander. Add the chicken slices, toss to coat them in the mixture, then stir-fry for 3–4 minutes. Add the sugar snap peas, baby corn and bean sprouts to the stir-fried mixture, and steam briefly. Stir in the noodles, toss lightly, and heat through.

4 Mix the cornstarch, soy sauce, lemon juice and sugar in a small bowl. Add to the wok, and simmer briefly to thicken the sauce. Serve the stir-fry at once, garnished with chopped cilantro.

Minted Yogurt Chicken

INGREDIENTS

8 chicken thighs, skinned
1 tablespoon clear honey
2 tablespoons fresh lime or lemon juice
2 tablespoons plain yogurt
2 tablespoons chopped fresh mint
salt and ground black pepper
shredded mint leaves, to garnish
new potatoes, and tomato and mint salad,
to serve

1 Slash the chicken thighs at intervals with a sharp knife. Mix the honey, citrus juice, yogurt and half the mint in a large bowl. Stir in salt and pepper to taste. Add the chicken to the bowl, turning the thighs to coat them in the mixture. Cover, and set aside to marinate for 30 minutes.

2 Preheat the broiler. Line the broiler pan with foil. Carefully transfer the chicken, with as much of the coating as possible, to the broiler rack. Broil for 15–20 minutes or until cooked through and golden brown, turning once.

3 Garnish the chicken with shredded mint leaves, and serve at once. New potatoes, tossed in melted butter and ground black pepper, make the perfect accompaniment, with a fresh tomato and mint salad garnish.

41

Salads For All Seasons

Maryland Salad

INGREDIENTS

4 corn cobs
4 chicken breasts, skinned and boned
1 tablespoon corn oil
8 ounces rindless unsmoked bacon strips
3 tablespoons butter, softened
4 ripe bananas
4 firm tomatoes, halved
1 escarole or butterhead lettuce, separated
into leaves
1 bunch watercress
ground black pepper

DRESSING

5 tablespoons peanut oil
1 tablespoon white wine vinegar
2 teaspoons maple syrup
2 teaspoons mild mustard
1 tablespoon water

SERVES 4

---

1 Make the dressing. Mix all the ingredients in a screw-top jar, close tightly, and shake to combine. Preheat the broiler or prepare the barbecue.

2 Leaving the husks on, cook the corn cobs in a large saucepan of lightly salted water for about 12–15 minutes, until the kernels are just tender.

3 Meanwhile, brush the chicken breasts with oil, season them lightly with black pepper, and broil or barbecue for 15 minutes or until cooked through, turning once. Broil or barbecue the bacon for about 8–10 minutes, until crisp and browned.

4 Drain the corn, brush the cobs with butter, and broil or barbecue them, with the whole peeled bananas and tomatoes, until lightly browned. Toss the salad leaves with the dressing in a bowl, then arrange on four large plates. Slice the hot chicken, and arrange it on the leaves, with the bacon, bananas, tomatoes, watercress and broiled corn.

French Chicken Salad

INGREDIENTS

1 chicken, about 4–4½ pounds
⅔ cup white wine
⅔ cup water
24 French bread slices, about ¼ inch thick
1 garlic clove, peeled
8 ounces green beans, trimmed and cut into short lengths
4 ounces young spinach leaves
2 celery stalks, thinly sliced
2 sun-dried tomatoes in oil, drained and torn into shreds
2 scallions, thinly sliced
whole chives and Italian parsley, to garnish

VINAIGRETTE DRESSING
2 tablespoons red wine vinegar
¾ cup olive oil
1 tablespoon whole-grain mustard
1 tablespoon clear honey
2 tablespoons chopped mixed fresh herbs
2 teaspoons finely chopped capers
salt and ground black pepper

SERVES 4

1 Preheat the oven to 375°F. Put the chicken in a large casserole with the wine and water. Roast for about 1½ hours or until tender. Set aside to cool in the liquid, then skin the chicken, remove the flesh from the carcass, and cut it into neat pieces.

2 Make the dressing. Mix the vinegar, oil, mustard, honey, herbs and capers in a screw-top jar, close tightly, and shake to combine. Season to taste.

3 Toast the French bread slices under the broiler or in the oven until dry and golden brown, then rub lightly with the garlic clove.

4 Bring a saucepan of lightly salted water to a boil, add the green beans, and cook for 4–6 minutes until the beans are crisp-tender. Drain, refresh under cold water, and drain again.

5 Discarding the stalks, tear the spinach into small pieces. Arrange on serving plates with the celery, beans, sun-dried tomatoes, chicken and scallions. Spoon the dressing over, and arrange the toasted croûtes on top. Serve the salad garnished with whole chives and Italian parsley.

Chinese-style Chicken Salad

Ingredients

½ cucumber, peeled, seeded and cut
    into matchsticks
1 teaspoon salt
4 chicken breasts, boned
4 tablespoons dark soy sauce
pinch of Chinese five-spice powder
½ teaspoon lemon juice
3 tablespoons sunflower oil
2 tablespoons sesame oil
1 tablespoon sesame seeds
2 tablespoons dry sherry
2 carrots, cut into matchsticks
8 scallions, shredded
4 cups bean sprouts

Sauce

4 tablespoons crunchy peanut butter
2 teaspoons lemon juice
2 teaspoons sesame oil
¼ teaspoon hot chili powder
1 scallion, finely chopped

Serves 4

1 Place the cucumber matchsticks in a colander, sprinkle with the salt, and cover with a weighted plate. Set the colander over a bowl, and allow to drain for 30 minutes.

2 Put the chicken breasts in a large saucepan. Pour in sufficient water to just cover them, then add 1 tablespoon of the soy sauce with the five-spice powder and the lemon juice. Bring to a boil, cover the pan, and simmer for 20 minutes, adding more water if necessary. Drain the chicken, and remove the skin. Slice the flesh into thin strips.

3 Heat the oils in a wok. Fry the sesame seeds for 30 seconds, then stir in the rest of the soy sauce with the sherry. Add the carrots. Toss over the heat for 2–3 minutes until just tender, then turn the contents of the wok into a bowl, and set aside.

4 Rinse the cucumber thoroughly, drain, and pat dry on paper towels. Add to the bowl with the scallions, bean sprouts and chicken strips. Mix lightly, cover, and refrigerate for about 1 hour, turning the mixture in the juices occasionally.

5 Make the sauce. Cream the peanut butter with the lemon juice, sesame oil and chili powder. Add enough hot water to make a paste, then stir in the scallion. Arrange the chicken mixture on a serving dish, and offer the sauce separately.

Chicken Liver, Bacon & Tomato Salad

Ingredients

8 ounces young spinach leaves, stalks removed

1 frisée lettuce, separated into leaves

7 tablespoons sunflower oil

6 ounces rindless unsmoked bacon strips, cut into pieces

3 slices of day-old bread, crusts removed, cut into fingers

1 pound chicken livers, trimmed

4 ounces cherry tomatoes

salt and ground black pepper

Serves 4

1 Mix the spinach leaves and frisée lettuce together in a salad bowl. Heat 4 tablespoons of the oil in a large frying pan, add the bacon, and cook for about 3–4 minutes until crisp. Remove with a fish slice or slotted spoon, and drain on paper towels.

2 Add the bread fingers to the bacon-flavored oil remaining in the frying pan. Fry until crisp and golden, turning frequently. Drain on paper towels.

3 Add the remaining oil to the pan. When hot, add the chicken livers, and fry briskly for 2–3 minutes. Turn the livers out over the salad leaves. Add the bacon, croûtons and tomatoes, season with salt and pepper, toss lightly, and serve.

Chicken & Fruit Salad

INGREDIENTS

4 tarragon or rosemary sprigs
2 chickens, about 4–4½ pounds each
5 tablespoons butter, softened
⅔ cup chicken broth
⅔ cup white wine
1 cup walnut halves
lettuce leaves
1 small cantaloupe melon, halved, seeded and
shaped into balls
1 pound seedless grapes or pitted cherries
salt and ground black pepper

DRESSING

2 tablespoons tarragon vinegar
½ cup light olive oil
2 tablespoons chopped mixed fresh herbs

SERVES 8

1 Preheat the oven to 400°F. Put the herb sprigs inside the chickens, and season with salt and pepper. Spread 2 tablespoons of the butter over each chicken, place them in a roasting pan, and pour the broth around them. Cover loosely with foil, and roast for 1½–2 hours until cooked through, basting every 30 minutes. Transfer the chickens to a platter, and allow to cool.

2 Add the wine to the juices remaining in the roasting pan. Place over the heat, and cook until syrupy, then strain the mixture into a pitcher. Heat the remaining butter in a small frying pan, and fry the walnuts until lightly browned.

3 Make the dressing. Whisk the vinegar and oil together. Blot the chicken juices with paper towels to remove fat from the surface, then whisk the juices into the dressing with the herbs. Add salt and pepper to taste.

4 Joint the chickens. Arrange them on a bed of lettuce, with the melon balls and the grapes or pitted cherries. Spoon over the herb dressing, sprinkle with the browned walnuts, and serve.

Broiled Chicken Salad with Lavender

INGREDIENTS

4 chicken breasts, boned
1 pound young spinach leaves
6 ounces lamb's lettuce
8 cherry tomatoes, halved
salt and ground black pepper
8–12 fresh lavender sprigs, to garnish
LAVENDER MARINADE
6 fresh lavender flowers
2 teaspoons finely grated orange rind
2 garlic cloves, crushed
2 teaspoons clear honey
salt
2 tablespoons olive oil
2 teaspoons chopped fresh thyme
2 teaspoons chopped fresh marjoram
POLENTA
¼ cup butter
3¾ cups light chicken broth
1 cup fine corn meal (polenta)

SERVES 4

1 Make the marinade. Strip the lavender flowers from the stems. Mix with the orange rind, garlic, honey and salt in a bowl. Add the oil and herbs, and mix well. Slash the chicken breasts at intervals with a sharp knife, cutting down deeply through the skin. Place on a plate, spread with the marinade, cover, and let marinate for at least 20 minutes.

2 Now make the polenta. Use a little of the butter to grease a shallow baking pan. Bring the chicken broth to a boil in a large saucepan. Add the corn meal in a steady stream, stirring constantly for 2–3 minutes until thick. Turn the cooked mixture into the prepared pan, level the surface, and allow to cool.

3 Preheat the broiler or prepare a barbecue. Drain the chicken, discarding the marinade, and broil for about 15 minutes or until cooked right through, turning once. Meanwhile, cut the polenta into neat 1 inch cubes. Heat the remaining butter in a large frying pan, and fry the polenta until golden.

4 Divide the salad leaves, cubes of polenta and cherry tomatoes among four large plates. Cut the chicken breasts diagonally into thick slices, and arrange one on each salad. Garnish each salad with 2 or 3 lavender sprigs, and serve at once.

Dinner Party Dishes

Chicken in Creamy Orange Sauce

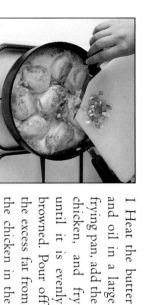

INGREDIENTS

SERVES 4

2 tablespoons butter
1 tablespoon corn oil
8 chicken thighs or drumsticks, skinned
3 tablespoons brandy
1¼ cups orange juice
3 scallions, chopped
2 teaspoons cornstarch mixed with
4 teaspoons water
6 tablespoons ricotta cheese
salt and ground black pepper
crushed black peppercorns, to garnish
rice or pasta, to serve

1 Heat the butter and oil in a large frying pan, add the chicken, and fry until it is evenly browned. Pour off the excess fat from the chicken in the pan, and add the brandy, orange juice and scallions. Bring to a boil, then lower the heat, cover the pan, and simmer for 20–30 minutes or until the chicken is cooked.

2 Stir the cornstarch mixture into the ricotta cheese in a small bowl. Add to the liquid in the pan, and stir over moderate heat until the sauce thickens. Add salt and pepper to taste. Serve sprinkled with crushed black peppercorns, accompanied by rice or pasta, garnished with fine shreds of orange rind, if liked.

Tender Chicken in Green Sauce

INGREDIENTS

2 tablespoons butter
1 tablespoon olive oil
4 chicken thighs, breasts or drumsticks, skinned
1 small onion, finely chopped
2/3 cup dry white wine
2/3 cup chicken broth
1 bunch watercress, leaves stripped from stalks
2 each thyme and tarragon sprigs, leaves stripped from stalks
2/3 cup heavy cream
salt and ground black pepper
boiled rice, to serve

SERVES 4

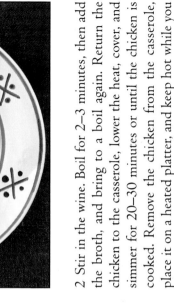

2 Stir in the wine. Boil for 2–3 minutes, then add the broth, and bring to a boil again. Return the chicken to the casserole, lower the heat, cover, and simmer for 20–30 minutes or until the chicken is cooked. Remove the chicken from the casserole, place it on a heated platter, and keep hot while you make the sauce.

3 Boil the cooking juices hard until reduced to about 4 tablespoons. Add the watercress and herb leaves. Stir in the cream, and simmer until slightly thickened. Return the chicken to the casserole, season with salt and pepper, and heat through for a few minutes. Serve with boiled rice.

1 Heat the butter and oil in a flame-proof casserole. Brown the chicken portions evenly, then transfer them to a plate, and set aside. Add the onion to the fat remaining in the casserole, and cook over low heat for 5 minutes until softened but not colored.

Tuscan Chicken

INGREDIENTS

SERVES 4

1 tablespoon olive oil
8 chicken thighs, skinned
1 onion, thinly sliced
2 red bell peppers, seeded and sliced
1 garlic clove, crushed
1¼ cups strained tomatoes
⅔ cup dry white wine
leaves from 1 large oregano sprig or
1 teaspoon dried oregano, plus extra fresh
oregano to garnish
14-ounce can cannellini beans, drained
3 tablespoons fresh white bread crumbs
salt and ground black pepper

1 Heat the oil in a large heavy-bottomed frying pan which can be used under the broiler. Fry the chicken thighs until brown on all sides. Transfer to a plate, and keep hot. Add the onion and peppers to the fat remaining in the pan, and sauté until the onion is softened but not browned.

2 Stir in the garlic, strained tomatoes, wine and oregano. Return the chicken thighs to the pan, and add salt and pepper to taste. Bring to a boil, lower the heat, and cover the pan tightly. Simmer for about 30 minutes, stirring occasionally, until the chicken is cooked through. Preheat the broiler.

3 Stir the cannellini beans into the pan. Re-cover, and simmer for 5 minutes until heated through.

4 Sprinkle the chicken mixture evenly with the bread crumbs. Place the pan under the broiler until the crumb topping is golden. Serve at once, garnished with oregano.

Chicken & Shrimp Jambalaya

INGREDIENTS

4 tablespoons shortening or bacon fat

2 chickens, about 3–3½ pounds each, jointed

1-pound piece raw smoked ham, rinded and diced

3 onions, finely sliced

½ cup flour

1½ pounds tomatoes, peeled and chopped, or 12 ounces canned chopped tomatoes

2 green bell peppers, seeded and sliced

2–3 garlic cloves, crushed

2 teaspoons chopped fresh thyme or 1 teaspoon dried thyme

3 cups long grain rice

5 cups water

2–3 dashes of Tabasco sauce

24 raw jumbo shrimp, peeled and deveined, tails left intact

1 bunch scallions, finely chopped (including the green tops)

3 tablespoons chopped fresh parsley

salt and ground black pepper

SERVES 8–10

1 Melt the shortening or bacon fat in a large heavy-bottomed frying pan or paella pan. Add the chicken pieces, diced ham and onions. Fry, turning occasionally, until the chicken pieces are golden brown on all sides. Using a slotted spoon, transfer the mixture to a dish, and set aside.

2 Lower the heat, sprinkle the flour into the fat left in the pan, and cook, stirring constantly, until the mixture is pale golden. Stir in the chopped tomatoes, green peppers, garlic and thyme. Cook, stirring, until the mixture forms a thick sauce, then return the chicken mixture to the pan, and cook for 10 minutes more, stirring occasionally.

3 Stir in the rice, with salt and pepper to taste. Pour in the water, add the Tabasco, and bring to a boil. Lower the heat, add the shrimp, and cook until the shrimp are pink, and the rice has absorbed the liquid and is tender.

4 Stir in the scallions with 2 tablespoons of the chopped parsley. Spoon the jambalaya onto a heated serving platter, garnish with the remaining chopped parsley, and serve at once.

Fragrant Chicken Curry

INGREDIENTS

½ cup red lentils
2 tablespoons mild curry powder
2 teaspoons ground coriander
1 teaspoon cumin seeds
2 cups vegetable broth
8 chicken thighs, skinned
8 ounces shredded or chopped spinach, thawed
and well drained if frozen
1 tablespoon chopped fresh cilantro
salt and ground black pepper
fresh cilantro sprigs, to garnish
white or brown basmati rice, poppadums and
cucumber and yogurt salad, to serve

SERVES 4

2 Add the chicken and spinach to the pan, replace the lid, and simmer gently for about 30 minutes more, or until the chicken is cooked, and the liquid has been absorbed. Season to taste.

3 Stir in the chopped cilantro. Garnish with fresh cilantro sprigs, and serve with basmati rice, poppadums and a cucumber and yogurt salad.

1 Place the lentils in a strainer, and rinse under cold running water. Drain well, turn into a large heavy-bottomed pan, and add the curry powder, ground coriander, cumin seeds and broth. Bring to a boil, lower the heat, cover, and simmer for 10 minutes.

Spatchcock of Squabs

INGREDIENTS

4 squabs

4 tablespoons butter, melted

1 tablespoon lemon juice

1 tablespoon chopped mixed fresh herbs, such as rosemary and parsley, plus extra to garnish

salt and ground black pepper

new potatoes and mixed salad, to serve

SERVES 4

1 Remove any trussing strings from the birds, and using a pair of kitchen scissors, cut down on each side of the back-bone. Lay the squabs flat, and flatten with the help of a rolling pin or mallet. Thread the legs and wings onto skewers to keep the squabs flat while they are cooking.

2 Preheat the broiler. Brush the squabs on both sides with melted butter, and season to taste. Sprinkle with lemon juice and herbs. Cook skin-side first for 6 minutes until golden. Turn over, brush with more butter, and broil for 6–8 minutes more or until cooked. Garnish with chopped herbs. Serve with new potatoes and mixed salad.

Lemon Chicken with Guacamole

INGREDIENTS

juice of 2 lemons
3 tablespoons olive oil
2 garlic cloves, finely chopped
4 chicken breasts, boned
2 large tomatoes, halved and cored
salt and ground black pepper
lettuce leaves and chopped fresh cilantro,
to garnish

SAUCE

1 ripe avocado
4 tablespoons sour cream
3 tablespoons lemon juice
½ teaspoon salt

SERVES 4

2 Make the sauce. Cut the avocado in half, remove the pit, and peel off the skin. Scrape the flesh into a food processor or blender. Add the sour cream, lemon juice and salt. Process until smooth. Add 4 tbsp water to the avocado mixture, and process for just long enough to combine. If the sauce is too thick, add a little more water. Scrape the sauce into a bowl, add salt and pepper to taste, and cover closely. Set aside in a cool place.

3 Heat a ridged frying pan on the stove or prepare the barbecue. Remove the chicken breasts from the marinade, and pat them dry with paper towels. Add the breasts to the hot pan, and cook them for about 10 minutes, turning frequently, until cooked through. Alternatively, barbecue the chicken on a lightly oiled grill over moderately hot coals.

4 Arrange the tomatoes on a baking sheet, season lightly, and broil or barbecue for 5 minutes.

5 Serve the chicken breasts on individual plates, with half a tomato and some guacamole dusted with chopped cilantro. Garnish with lettuce, and serve any remaining guacamole in a separate bowl.

1 Combine the lemon juice, oil and garlic in a bowl. Add ½ teaspoon salt, and mix well. Arrange the chicken breasts in a single layer in a shallow glass or ceramic dish. Pour over the lemon mixture, and turn to coat evenly. Cover, and set aside for 1 hour at room temperature, or refrigerate overnight.

Chicken Packages with Herb Butter

INGREDIENTS

4 chicken breasts, skinned and boned
⅔ cup butter, softened
6 tablespoons chopped fresh herbs
1 teaspoon lemon juice
5 large sheets of filo pastry, thawed if frozen
beaten egg, to glaze
2 tablespoons grated Parmesan cheese
salt and ground black pepper
fresh thyme sprigs, to garnish
salad leaves, to serve

SERVES 4

1 Preheat the oven to 375°F. Grease a baking sheet. Season the chicken breasts. Melt 2 tablespoons of the butter in a frying pan, add the chicken, and brown lightly on all sides. Remove from the pan, and allow to cool.

2 Cream the remaining butter with the herbs and lemon juice. Melt half the herb butter in the frying pan. Keeping the remainder of the filo covered, brush one sheet with melted butter. Fold the filo sheet in half, and brush again with butter, then place a chicken breast about 1 inch from the top.

3 Dot the chicken with a quarter of the remaining herb butter, fold in the sides, then roll the chicken breast up in the filo to enclose it completely. Place seam-side down on the prepared baking sheet. Make three more packages in the same way.

4 Brush the filo packages with some of the beaten egg. Cut the remaining sheet of filo into strips, scrunch them up, and arrange them on top. Brush again with beaten egg, and sprinkle with Parmesan. Bake for 35–40 minutes, until golden brown. Serve at once with salad leaves, garnished with thyme.

Cornish Game Hens Veronique

INGREDIENTS

2 tarragon or thyme sprigs
2 x 2-pound Cornish game hens
2 tablespoons butter
4 tablespoons white wine
grated rind and juice of ½ lemon
1 tablespoon olive oil
1 tablespoon flour
⅔ cup chicken broth
4 ounces seedless green grapes, halved if large
salt and ground black pepper
tarragon sprigs and chopped fresh parsley,
to garnish
green beans, to serve

1 Preheat the oven to 350°F. Tuck the herbs inside the game hens, then tie each bird into a neat shape. Heat the butter in a flameproof casserole, brown the birds lightly all over, and pour on the wine. Season, transfer the casserole to the oven, and cook the birds for 20–30 minutes until tender.

2 Preheat the broiler. Remove the game hens from the casserole, and cut each bird in half with a pair of poultry shears, removing the backbones and small rib cage bones. Arrange on a shallow, flameproof dish. Sprinkle with the lemon juice, and brush with the oil. Broil until lightly browned, then transfer to a heated platter, and keep hot.

3 Sprinkle the flour over the juices remaining in the casserole. Stir until smooth, then stir in the broth. Bring to a boil, stirring. Add salt and pepper to taste, and fold in the lemon rind and grapes. Simmer for 2–3 minutes. Spoon the sauce over the game hens, garnish with tarragon sprigs and chopped parsley, and serve with green beans.

Index